My Chri Fun Book

In My Own Words
All About Me

Written by Faye Deaton Brophy and Sharon Gordon
Illustrated by Faye Deaton Brophy

Tell your story!
Just fill in the blanks using words,
pictures, or photos.

This book belongs to _____

This book was given by _____

Date _____

Troll Associates

Christmas season is a wonderful time of the year.

To me, Christmas means _____ and _____.
If I could make one thing about Christmas last all year long,
it would be _____.

These are some of the things that really put me in the
Christmas spirit: _____
_____

I have a lot of fun with my family around Christmas. These are
some of the things we do together to celebrate: _____
_____
_____

Here are the names and ages of the people in my family:
_____
_____

Here is a picture of me and my family.

(Use this space to draw a picture
or paste in a photo.)

Our Christmas Tree

I love a Christmas tree! We usually put our Christmas tree in _____. Once we had a tree that was _____ feet tall and _____ feet wide. We usually decorate our Christmas tree with _____, _____, and _____. I like the job of putting the _____ on the tree because _____ _____.

Once I made a _____ to hang on the Christmas tree. We have Christmas tree balls that are these colors: _____.

But my favorite color is _____.

I love the way the Christmas tree smells. It smells like _____. This is a picture of our Christmas tree this year.

My Stocking

This is where I like to hang my Christmas stocking:
_____ . Once I put a
_____ in a Christmas stocking for
_____ .
These are the things that I like to find inside my
Christmas stocking: _____
_____ .
I'd like to have a Christmas stocking the size of a
_____ , so that it could be filled with
a _____ .
Here is a Christmas stocking decorated just like *my*
Christmas stocking.

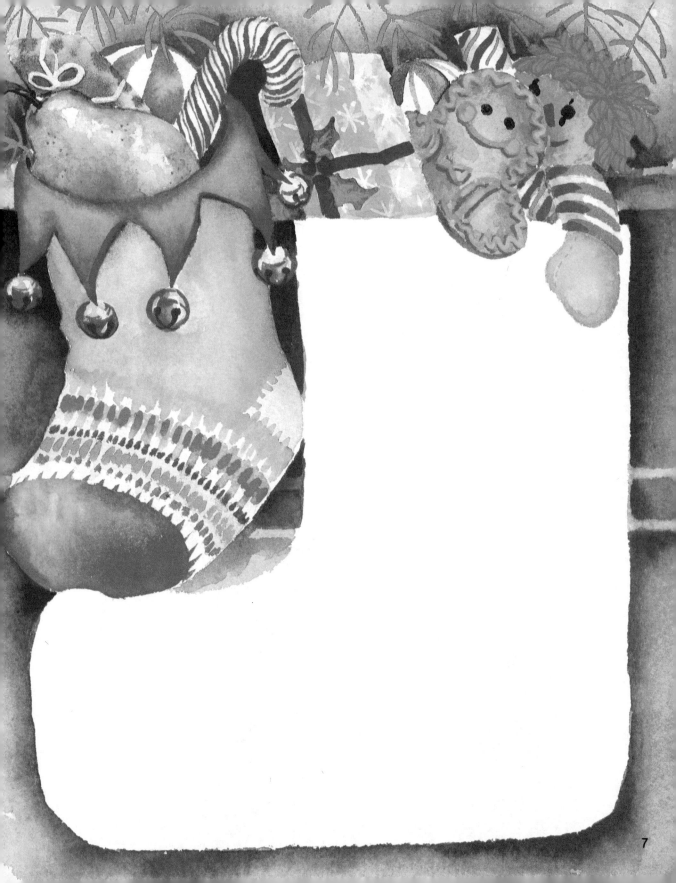

My Christmas Presents

The best Christmas present I ever received was a _____.
The person who gave it to me was _____ .
The strangest Christmas present I ever received was a
_____ from _____ .
This is what I said when I saw it: " _____
_____ ."
This is the present I would like to get on Christmas: _____
_____ .

If I could buy anything in the world for my family and friends at Christmas, these are the gifts I would give them:

_____

_____

_____

This is a picture of the present I would like.

Draw here

Santa's Helper

I would love to be Santa's helper.
First I would help him _____
and together we would fly to

_____

and _____ ,
delivering presents. I would
wave hello to _____
as we flew over the town of

_____ .

Later, we would fly back to the
North Pole, where I would help
Santa _____ and

_____ .

Then we would share some
_____ and

eat delicious _____ .

My photo or picture

Here is a picture of Santa and his best helper—me!

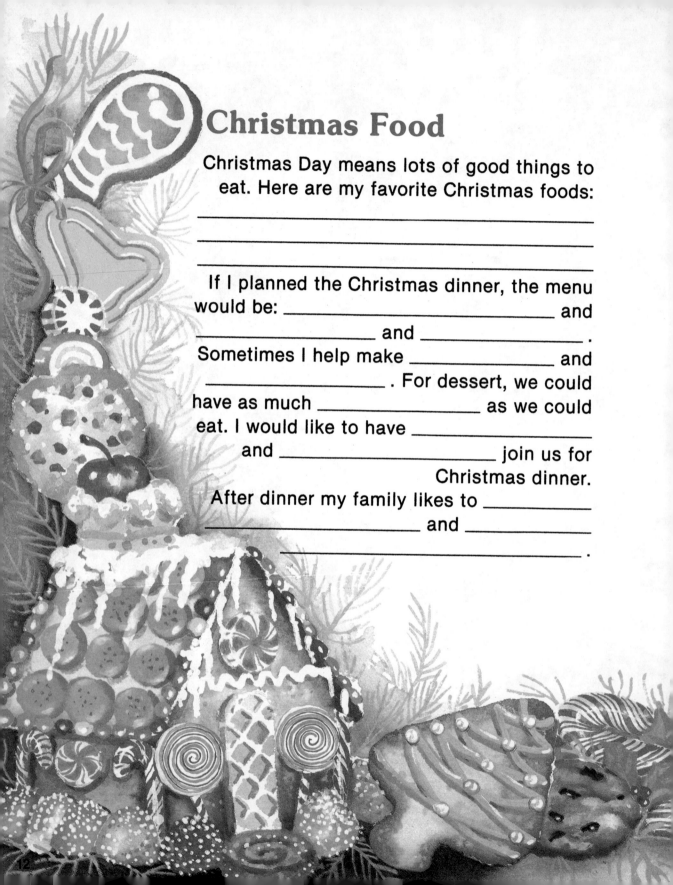

Christmas Food

Christmas Day means lots of good things to eat. Here are my favorite Christmas foods:

_____

_____

_____

If I planned the Christmas dinner, the menu would be: _____ and _____ and _____ . Sometimes I help make _____ and _____ . For dessert, we could have as much _____ as we could eat. I would like to have _____ and _____ join us for Christmas dinner. After dinner my family likes to _____ _____ and _____ _____ .

Here is a picture of me
eating my favorite Christmas food.

My Christmas Costume Party

It would be lots of fun to have a Christmas party where everyone came dressed as different Christmas characters. These are the people I would invite: _____

_____

_____

_____

_____

My friend _____ would look great dressed as _____ . I would wear a _____ costume. Here is a picture of how I would look.

These are some of the games we might play: _____

_____ .

Snowflakes

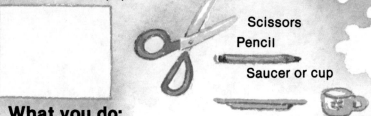

What you need:

White or colored paper

Scissors
Pencil
Saucer or cup

What you do:

1 Trace around any circular object (saucer, cup, etc.) the size of the snowflake you want.

2 Cut out the circle.

3 Fold in half, then in thirds, and then in half again.

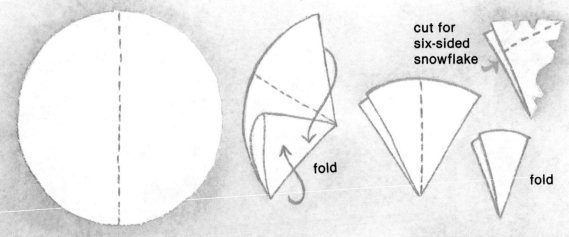

cut for six-sided snowflake

fold

fold

4 Draw a design like the ones below, or make a design of your own.

16

5 Carefully cut out the design and open slowly. Be careful not to tear it.

Your snowflakes can be used to decorate many things. Make a paper placemat, and glue snowflakes in place. Attach snowflakes to your window. Tape them onto your Christmas presents. Glue them onto your Christmas cards.

Christmas Time Traveler

I think it would
be fun to travel
through time
to see what
Christmas would
be like far in the
future, or far in
the past.

For my trip
into the future,
I would travel
ahead in time to
the year _____
to visit _____ .
These are the things I might
see and do on Christmas
day: _____
_____
_____ .

For my trip into the past, I would go back to the year _____ . These are the things I might see and do on Christmas Day:

_____

_____ .

But after traveling to different times and places, I still think Christmas is best here and now because _____

_____ .

A Silly Santa Story

I always enjoy hearing how Santa Claus and his reindeer bring presents to people all over the world. But I think it would be funny if, one year, things happened a little differently. Here is what might happen.

    I think Santa was very mixed up this year. First of all, he was late. Instead of coming at _____ o'clock, he arrived _____ . And instead of eight reindeer pulling his sleigh, there were eight _____ doing the job!
    Then, I saw Santa trying to come in through the _____ instead of the chimney. Here is a picture of how he looked.

The funniest thing of all was that Santa Claus was not wearing his usual outfit. Instead of a red suit, he was wearing a _____ , with a _____ on his head and _____ on his feet.

He wore _____ around his waist. He carried his presents in a _____ .

When Santa saw our Christmas stockings, he put _____ in them instead of presents. As he was leaving, he said, " _____ ! And have a very merry Christmas!" What a funny Santa Claus! This is a picture of how Santa was dressed.

Three Christmas Cookies

Gingerbread Men

What you need:

  2 cups flour

 1/3 cup sugar

Rolling Pin

Bowl

Cookie sheet

1/2 cup shortening

1/2 cup molasses

1 teaspoon baking powder
1 teaspoon baking soda
1 teaspoon cinnamon
1/2 teaspoon ginger
3 tablespoons hot water

Cookie cutter

What you do:

1 With an adult's help, combine all ingredients in a large bowl. Blend well.

2 Chill dough at least one hour.

3 Roll out dough on floured surface to 1/8 inch thickness. Use gingerbread man cookie cutter.

4 Place on ungreased cookie sheet. Bake at 400° for eight to ten minutes. Cool and decorate.

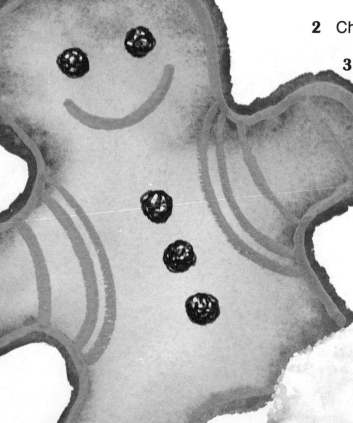

Snowballs

What you need:

 2½ cups flour

1 cup softened butter

½ cup confectioner's sugar

¾ cup chopped walnuts

1 teaspoon vanilla

Cookie sheet

What you do:

1 With an adult's help, heat oven to 350°.

2 Stir butter, sugar, nuts, and vanilla together. Mix well.

3 Roll batter into one-inch balls with your hands.

4 Place balls on cookie sheet and bake ten minutes.

5 After cookies cool, roll them in additional confectioner's sugar to make the snowball.

Christmas Kisses

What you need:

 4 egg whites

 ½ teaspoon vanilla

Pinch of salt

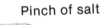 1 cup of sugar

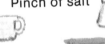 Bowl

1 cup chopped nuts

Waxed paper

 Cookie sheet

Extra nuts

What you do:

1 With an adult's help, separate the egg whites from the yolks. In a large bowl, beat the egg whites until stiff.

2 Add sugar, salt, and vanilla. Continue beating until sugar is mixed in.

3 Stir in the nuts.

4 Cover a cookie sheet with waxed paper, and drop the batter onto the sheet in small mounds with a teaspoon.

5 Decorate each cookie with a nut.

6 Bake at 300° for about twenty minutes. Makes about forty-five kisses.

My Christmas Clay

What fun you will have making your own Christmas decorations and ornaments!

What you need:

1 cup flour   ¼ cup salt   wooden spoon   Mixing bowl   Water-base paints

Rolling pin   ⅓ cup water   Plastic wrap   Paper clips   Clear polish   Colored yarn

Brush   Wax paper

What you do:

1   Put the flour, salt, and water in a bowl.

2   Mix well with spoon. Press clay between your fingers to get out lumps. If clay feels dry, add a few drops of water. If too mushy, add flour.

3   Store in plastic bag in refrigerator.

4   Make simple figures. If you like, roll out clay on wax paper. Use cookie cutters to make the shapes you want.

5   While the ornaments are still soft, press a paper clip into the top of each one. Make sure the top of the clip extends over the top of the figure.

6 Let the figures dry for two or three days, or bake at 350°
(one-half hour for smaller figures and one hour for heavier figures).

7 Color them with paint, and then varnish with polish.

8 Decorate with glitter if you wish.

9 String yarn through the paper clip loops, and hang your ornaments
on your Christmas tree.

(Note: a sieve or garlic press can be used to make hair.)

My Holly Wreath

What you need:

Green and red construction paper

 Paper plate

 Dime

 Pencil

Scissors

 Glue

 Red ribbon (optional)

What you do:

1 Cut out the center of the paper plate.

2 On green paper, copy this holly leaf pattern. Trace as many leaves as will fit on your paper. Carefully cut them out. Your leaves should have sharp points.

3 Glue leaves to the plate. Overlap them to completely cover the plate.

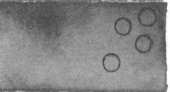

4 Make small berries by tracing around a dime.

5 Cut out berries, and glue in bunches of three to the wreath.

6 Add a bow made of red paper, or use ribbon. A red bow is pretty.

7 Hang your wreath in a window or decorate a wall or door.

My Christmas Stocking

What you need:

Straight pins

Glue

Scissors

Heavy paper

Piece of red felt twice as big as the stocking you are planning

Needle

Crayon

Decorations: yarn, sequins, scraps of felt, rickrack

What you do:

1 Draw a pattern for the stocking on a piece of heavy paper.

2 Cut out the pattern. Pin it to a piece of red felt that has been folded in half.

3 Carefully cut around the pattern. You will have two stocking-shaped pieces of felt.

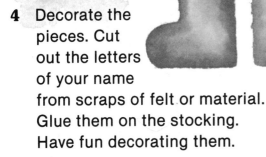

4 Decorate the pieces. Cut out the letters of your name from scraps of felt or material. Glue them on the stocking. Have fun decorating them.

5 After decorating both sides, use a piece of heavy yarn to make a handle. Glue it to the wrong side of one stocking piece.

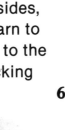

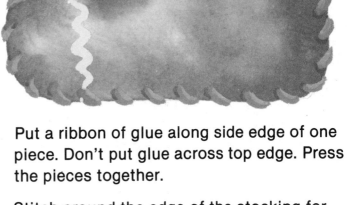

6 Put a ribbon of glue along side edge of one piece. Don't put glue across top edge. Press the pieces together.

7 Stitch around the edge of the stocking for extra strength.

My Christmas Cards

One of the funniest Christmas cards I ever received was from
_____ . It had a picture of _____
on the front, and the message inside read " _____
_____ ."
I would like to send a special Christmas card to this person:
_____.
It would really be great if I got Christmas cards from my
friends: _____ ,
and from this famous person: _____.
This is a Christmas card that I designed:

Here are some ideas for your Christmas cards. Have fun making new designs.

What you need:

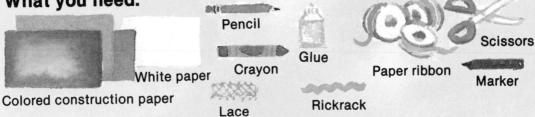

White paper

Colored construction paper

Pencil

Crayon

Glue

Paper ribbon

Scissors

Marker

Lace

Rickrack

What you do:

1 Fold a sheet of construction paper in half.

2 Paint or draw designs on your cards.

3 Tear or cut shapes from colored paper, and glue onto card.

4 Cut different lengths or chips of ribbon, and glue onto card.

5 Write your Christmas message inside with marker or pencil.

Merry Christmas

Happy New Year

Here is what a happy New Year means to me: _____

_____.

It would be wonderful if these things happened to me this year: _____

_____

This is a New Year's resolution that I kept: _____

_____.

A New Year's resolution that I didn't keep was:

_____

_____

_____

Here is a list of New Year's resolutions that I will *try* to keep this year: _____

_____

_____

_____

_____

_____

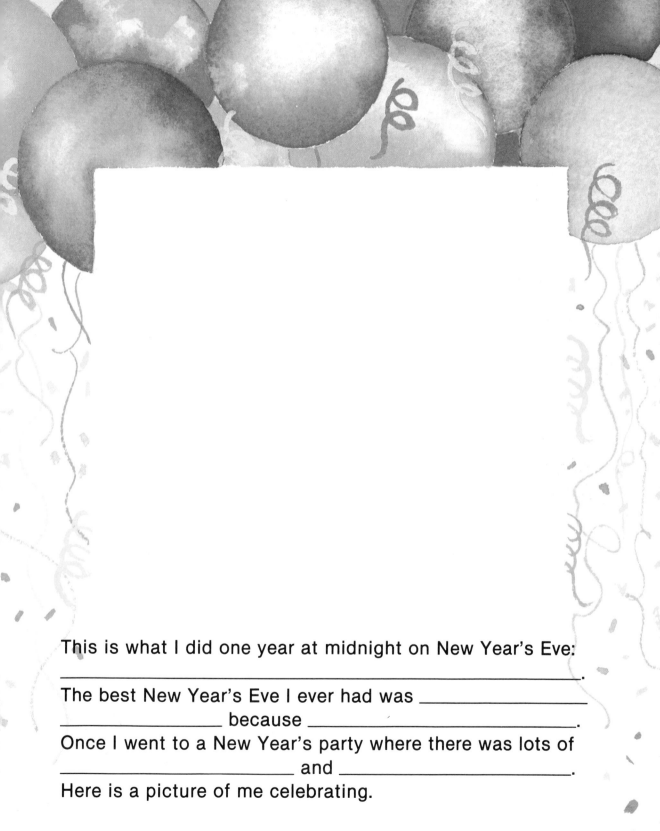

This is what I did one year at midnight on New Year's Eve:

_____.

The best New Year's Eve I ever had was _____

_____ because _____.

Once I went to a New Year's party where there was lots of

_____ and _____.

Here is a picture of me celebrating.

Here are some things that would make my New Year very happy:

Meeting this person: _____

Traveling to _____

Going to this movie _____

Going to this concert _____

Seeing this sport _____

Getting an "A" in _____

Learning to _____

Taking a _____

Finding the _____

Fixing up my _____

Making a _____

Discovering _____

Reading _____

Growing a _____

Building a _____

Reading about _____

Here is a picture of me!